Herbert Puchta Günter Gerngross Peter Lewis-Jones

Super Minds

Student's Book Starter

CAMBRIDGE
UNIVERSITY PRESS

Map of the book

Hello (pages 4–9)

Vocabulary	Grammar	Story and value	Thinking skills
red, blue, green, orange, purple, yellow	Hello! What's your name? I'm ...	**The water hole** Saying Sorry	Associating silhouettes with objects

▶ **Song:** What's your name?

1 My classroom (pages 10–19)

Vocabulary	Grammar	Story and value	Thinking skills	English for school
• pencil, chair, bag, rubber, book, desk • one, two, three, four, five, six	Stand up. Sit down. Open ... Close ... Pick up ... Put ...	**The pencil** Lending	• Counting • Paying attention to visual details • Associating objects with actions	Actions at school

▶ **Song:** In the classroom   ▶ **Creativity**   ▶ **Revision**

2 My family (pages 20–29)

Vocabulary	Grammar	Story and value	Thinking skills	English for school
grandpa, grandma, mum, dad, sister, brother	• This is my (brother), (Tom). • This is my (book).	**The sandwiches** Sharing	• Counting • Understanding family relations	**Social science:** Families

▶ **Song:** We're the royal family!   ▶ **Creativity**   ▶ **Revision**

3 My face (pages 30–39)

Vocabulary	Grammar	Story and value	Thinking skills	English for school
eyes, ears, nose, face, teeth, mouth	• I'm/You're (angry, happy, sad, scared). • Are you (angry)? Yes, I am. / No, I'm not.	**The monster** Don't play tricks	• Comparing and analysing visual information • Empathising with others	**Music:** Music and feelings

▶ **Song:** Hey, little clown   ▶ **Creativity**   ▶ **Revision**

4 Toys (pages 40–49)

Vocabulary	Grammar	Story and value	Thinking skills	English for school
• ball, kite, rope, teddy bear, doll, plane • seven, eight, nine, ten	I've got a (ball).	**The ball** Working together	• Counting • Paying attention to visual details	**Physical education:** Let's play outside!

▶ **Song:** I've got a ball   ▶ **Creativity**   ▶ **Revision**

⑤ My house (pages 50–59)

Vocabulary	Grammar	Story and value	Thinking skills	English for school
bath, cupboard, bed, sofa, table, armchair	• in, on, under • The (doll) is in the (bath).	**The cap** Listening to people	• Paying attention to visual details • Paying attention to details in instructions	**Geography:** Homes

▶ **Song:** Tidy up! ▶ **Creativity** ▶ **Revision**

⑥ On the farm (pages 60–69)

Vocabulary	Grammar	Story and value	Thinking skills	English for school
cat, horse, cow, dog, rabbit, sheep	• (two) sheep, three (cat)s, I like (cats) • My favourite colour is (blue) / (toys) are (planes).	**I like your colours!** Paying compliments	• Counting • Remembering details from a story • Associating animals with habitats	**Biology:** Animals

▶ **Song:** The animal boogie ▶ **Creativity** ▶ **Revision**

⑦ I'm hungry! (pages 70–79)

Vocabulary	Grammar	Story and value	Thinking skills	English for school
carrots, sausages, apples, cakes, ice cream, chips	• I like / don't like (carrots). • I like / I don't like (blue / cats / dolls).	**Cakes and ice cream** Don't be greedy	• Identifying missing details • Associating food with its source	**Science:** Our food

▶ **Song:** I don't like chips ▶ **Creativity** ▶ **Revision**

⑧ All aboard! (pages 80–89)

Vocabulary	Grammar	Story and value	Thinking skills	English for school
boat, train, car, scooter, bus, bike	• I'm driving / flying / riding / sailing • flying a kite, swimming, climbing a tree, running, brushing my teeth, washing my hands	**Oh what fun!** Saying Thank you	• Associating sound clues with silhouettes • Paying attention to visual details • Recognising shapes • Counting	**Maths:** Shapes

▶ **Song:** We're having fun! ▶ **Creativity** ▶ **Revision**

⑨ Party clothes (pages 90–99)

Vocabulary	Grammar	Story and value	Thinking skills	English for school
hat, belt, boots, shirt, badge, shoes	• I like (biscuits, crisps, salad, sweets). • I've got (apples and salad / a ball).	**Nice work!** Tidying up	• Ranking in order of preference • Associating outlines with objects • Paying attention to visual details • Recognising numbers	**Art:** Our clothes

▶ **Song:** Oh what a wonderful party! ▶ **Creativity** ▶ **Revision**

Chants and songs: pages 100–102   **Cut-outs:** pages 103–112   **Stickers:** Centre section

Hello

1 CD1 02 **Listen and sing.**

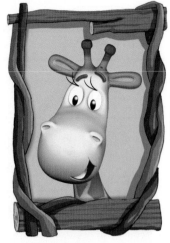

2 CD1 05 **Listen and point.**

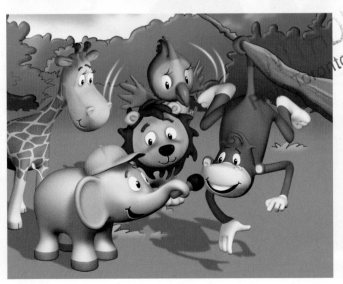

1 Act out.

Pages 110–112

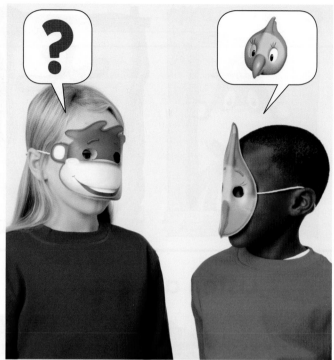

2 Ask and answer.

I'm (Mike, Leo, Gina, Polly).

1 CD1 07 **Listen and point.**

2 **Move a CD. Look and say the colours.**

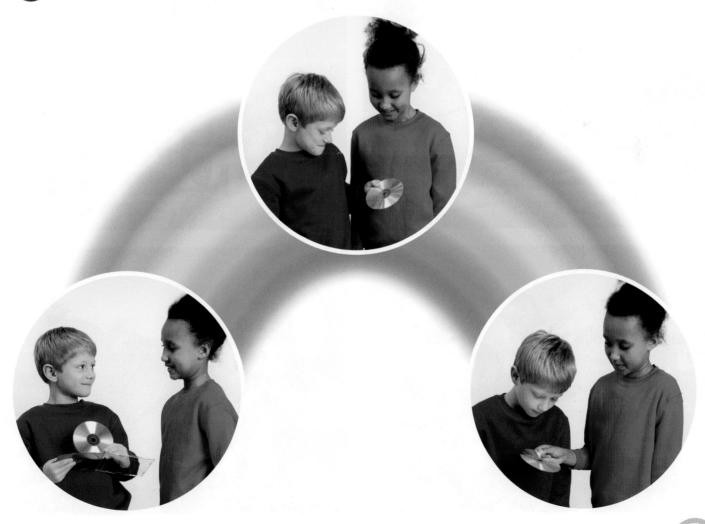

The water hole

2 Think! **Find and say the colour.**

1 My classroom

1 CD1 10 Listen and point. Then listen and say the words.

2 CD1 11 Listen and chant.

1 pencil 2 chair 3 bag 4 rubber 5 book 6 desk

1 CD1 12 Listen and colour.

1

2

3

4

5

6

2 CD1 13 Listen and act out.

Stand up. Sit down. Open ... Close ... Pick up ... Put ...

Listen and sing.

1 **CD1 17** **Listen and say the numbers.**

2 Think! **Look and count. Circle the number.**

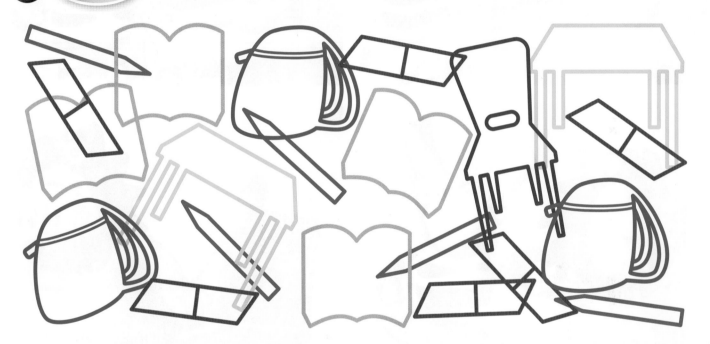

📖	1	2	3	4	5	6
✏️	1	2	3	4	5	6
👜	1	2	3	4	5	6
🪑	1	2	3	4	5	6
▱	1	2	3	4	5	6
🪑	1	2	3	4	5	6

one, two, three, four, five, six   13

The pencil

2 Think! Sticker   Find, count and stick.

1

2

3

4

5

6

Actions at school

1 Listen and say the words.

2 Play the game.

1 (Think!) **Think and colour.**

1

2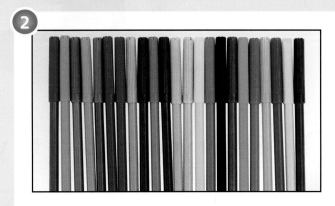

3

4

5

6

Listen and imagine. Then draw your picture.

2 **Show your picture to your friends.**

1 Play the game.

2 My family

2 CD1 24 **Listen and chant.**

20 1 grandpa 2 grandma 3 mum 4 dad 5 sister 6 brother

1 **Listen, point and say the words.**

2 **Draw and show your family. Say the names.**

This is my (brother), (Tom). 21

1 Follow the lines. Make sentences.

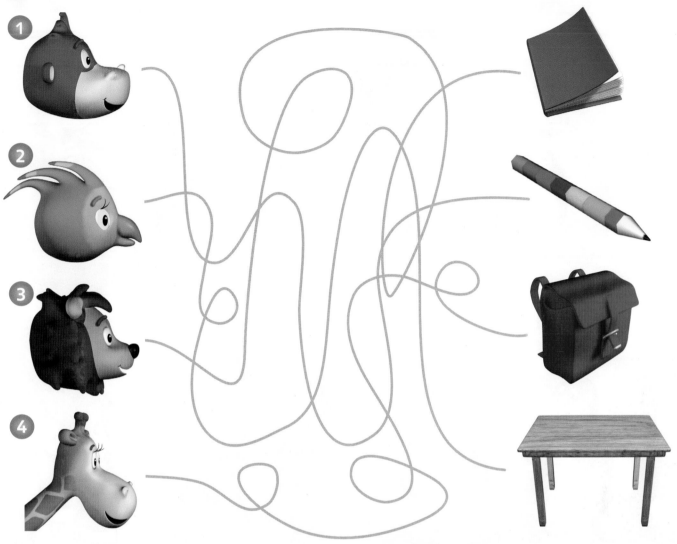

2 Play the game.

This is my (book). 23

The sandwiches

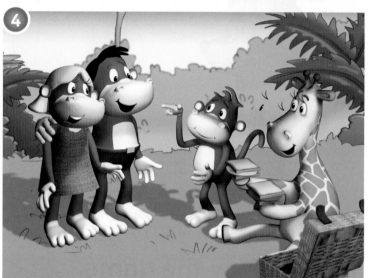

2 Think! **Count and colour.**

Families

1 CD1 31 **Think!** **Listen and stick.**

Sticker

2 **Draw and show your family tree.**

1 **Make a finger family.**

2 **Show your family to a friend.**

1 Listen and act out with your teacher.

 2 Listen again and match.

 **1**    **2**    **3**

 **4**    **5**    **6**

1 ✂ Page 108

Play the game.

③ My face

2 CD1 35 **Listen and chant.**

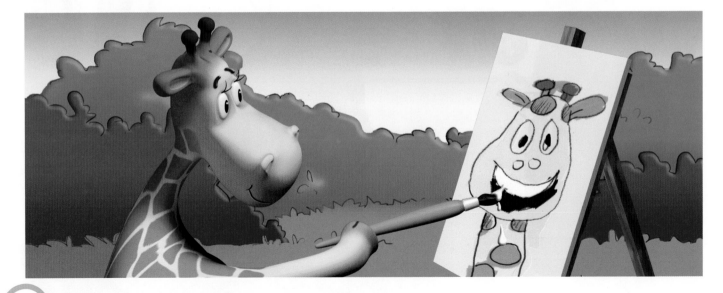

30 | 1 eyes 2 ears 3 nose 4 face 5 teeth 6 mouth

1 CD1 36 Listen and say the words.

2 Play the game.

I'm/You're (angry, happy, sad, scared).   31

1 CD1 37 **Listen and sing.**

1 CD1 39 Sticker **Listen and stick.**

2 **Draw a face. Play the game.**

Are you (angry)? Yes, I am. / No, I'm not. **33**

2 (Think!) **Look at picture 4. Find five differences.**

Music and feelings

1 ^{CD1 43} Listen and colour. Say the words.

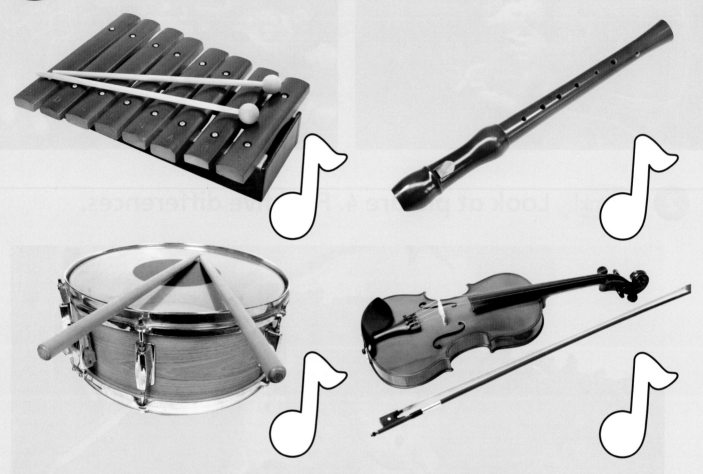

2 ^{CD1 44} Listen again and describe the music.

1 CD1 45 **Think!** **Listen and circle.**

1 2 3 4

1 2 3 4

1 2 3 4

1 2 3 4

2 **Play the game.**

1 **Listen and imagine. Then make a face.**

2 **Show the face to your friends.**

1 Play the game.

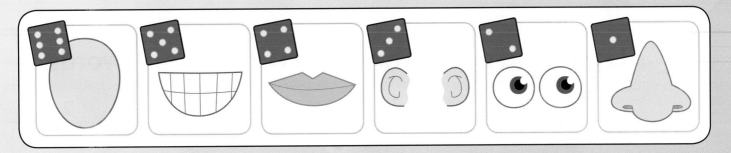

4 Toys

1 CD1 47 **Listen and point. Then listen and say the words.**

2 CD1 48 **Listen and chant.**

1 ball 2 kite 3 rope 4 teddy bear 5 doll 6 plane

1 CD1 49 Listen and colour.

2 Choose three stickers and play the game.

Sticker

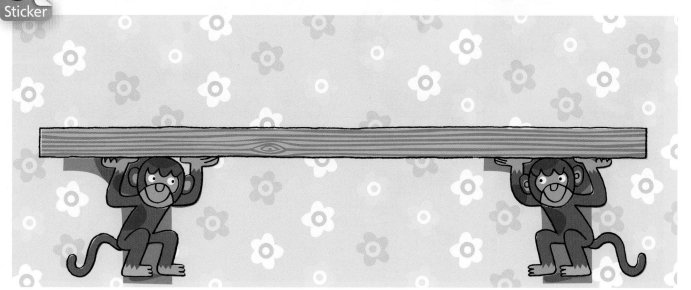

1 Listen and sing.

1 CD1 52 **Listen and say the numbers.**

2 Think! **Look and count. Circle the number.**

🪁	1	2	3	4	5	6	7	8	9	10
🏐	1	2	3	4	5	6	7	8	9	10
🪆	1	2	3	4	5	6	7	8	9	10
🧸	1	2	3	4	5	6	7	8	9	10
✈️	1	2	3	4	5	6	7	8	9	10
🪢	1	2	3	4	5	6	7	8	9	10

The ball

1

2

3

4

5

6

44 Story and values

2 Think! Look and draw the ball and the stick.

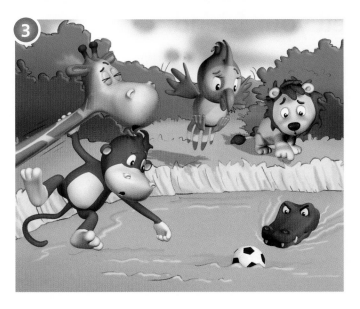

Let's play outside!

Listen. Point and say the number.

2 **Choose a picture and tell your friend.**

1 CD1 57 Listen and say the words.

1

2

3

4

5

6

2 CD1 58 Listen and act out.

1 Listen and act out with your teacher.

 2 Listen again and match.

 **1**  **2**  **3**

 **4**  **5**  **6**

48 Creativity

Play the game.

1

✂ Page 106

5 My house

1 CD2 02 **Listen and point. Then listen and say the words.**

1 bath
2 cupboard
3 bed
4 sofa
5 table
6 armchair

2 CD2 03 **Listen, chant and colour.**

bath, cupboard, bed, sofa, table, armchair

1 CD2 04 Listen and point. Then listen and answer.

1

on the bed

2

in the bath

3

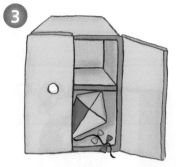

in the cupboard

4

under the armchair

5

under the table

6

on the sofa

2 Think! Find the toys.

1 Sticker **Make a picture with stickers.**

2 Sticker **Think!** **Describe your picture.**
Make your friend's picture.

The (doll) is (in) the (bath). 53

The cap

1

2

3

4

5

6

Story and values

2 Think! Find and say the picture number.

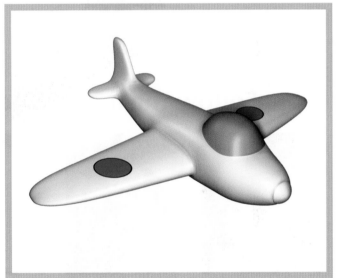

Homes

1
2
3
4
5

2 **Follow the lines. Where do the people live?**

1
2
3
4
5

1 **Choose a home. Use rubbish to make it.**

1 CD2 12 **Listen and imagine. Then draw your picture.**

2 **Show your picture to your friends.**

1 Play the game.

6 On the farm

1 CD2 13 **Listen and point. Then listen and say the words.**

← 1 cat

2 horse

3 cow

4 dog

5 rabbit

6 sheep

2 CD2 14 **Listen and chant.**

1 **Think!** **Count the animals.**

5 dogs

1 dogs
2 sheep
3 cats
4 cows
5 rabbits
6 horses

2 CD2 15 **Listen and stick.**

Sticker

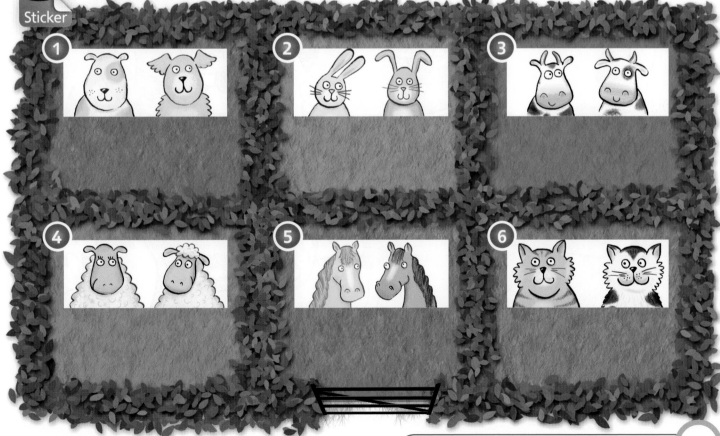

1 CD2 19 Listen and circle.

My favourite colour is blue.

I like cats.

2 Talk in class and count.

 # I like your colours!

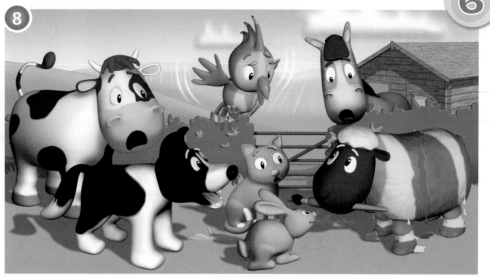

2 Think! Remember and circle the parts of the face.

Animals

1 **Make a poster.**

1 Play the game.

7 I'm hungry!

1 CD2 25 **Listen and point. Then listen and say the words.**

1 carrots

2 sausages

3 apples

4 cakes

5 ice cream

6 chips

2 CD2 26 **Listen and chant.**

carrots, sausages, apples, cakes, ice cream, chips

1 Listen and circle.

2 Talk about food.

I like apples.

I don't like sausages.

I like / I don't like (carrots).

1 **Listen to your teacher. True or false?**

2 **Play the game.**

↓→	1	2	3	4	5	6
1						
2						
3						
4						
5						
6						

I like / I don't like (blue / cats / dolls). **73**

Cakes and ice cream

1

2

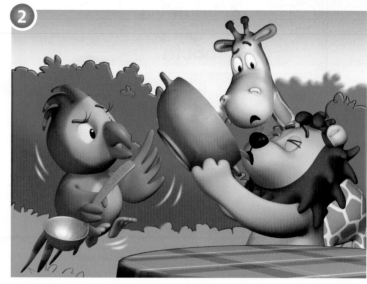

3

4

5

6

2 Think! Look and stick.

Sticker

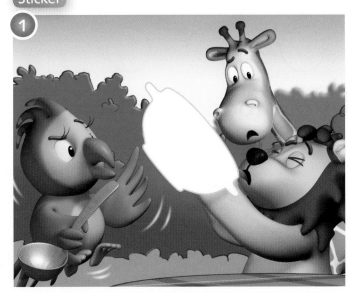

Our food

1 CD2 33 **Listen and colour.**

○　　○　　○

○　　○　　○

2 Think! **Match. Where does our food come from?**

1  **2**  **3**  **4**

1 Make food collages.

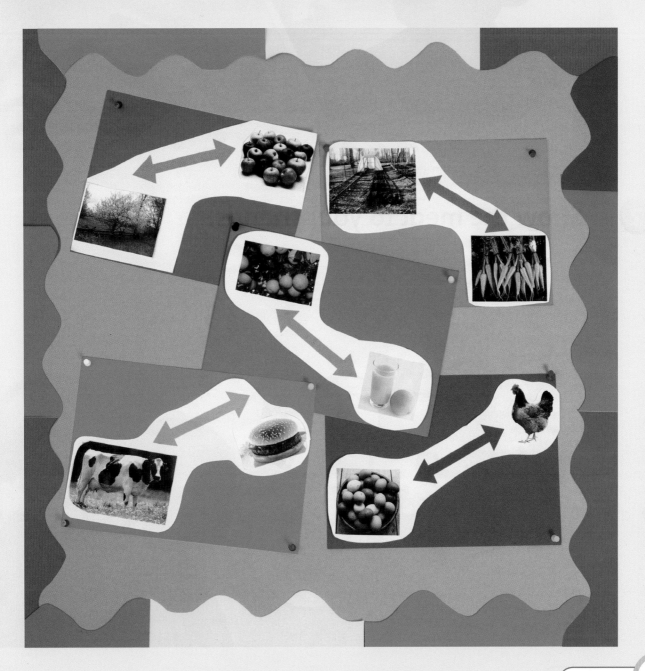

1 CD2 34 **Listen and imagine.
Then make a meal for your monster.**

2 **Show the meal to your friends.**

1 Play the game.

Page 104

8 All aboard!

Listen and point. Then listen and say the words.

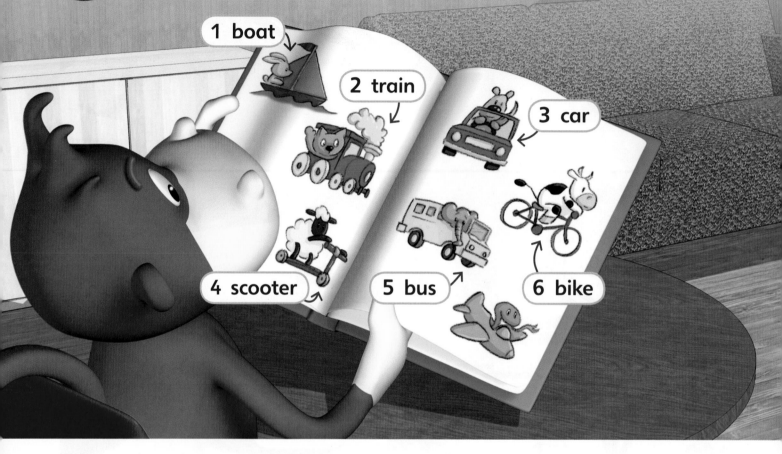

1 boat
2 train
3 car
4 scooter
5 bus
6 bike

2 CD2 36 Listen and chant.

boat, train, car, scooter, bus, bike

Listen and colour.

2 Play the game.

Are you riding a scooter?

1 CD2 41 **Think!** Listen, look and say the actions.

1

2

3

4

5

6

1 🪁 I'm flying a kite.

2 Sticker Look at activity 1 and stick.

flying a kite, swimming, climbing a tree, running, brushing my teeth, washing my hands

Oh what fun!

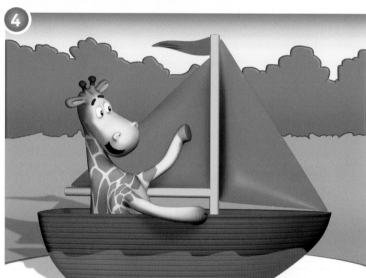

Story and values

2 **Think!** **Look, draw and colour.**

1

2

3

4

Shapes

1 CD2 45 **Listen and colour.**

1

2

3

4

2 Think! **Find shapes in the classroom.**

1 Think! Count the shapes.

1

2

3

4

2 Make a picture. Show the picture to your friends.

1 **Listen and act out with your teacher.**

2 **Listen again and match.**

 1 2 3

4 5 6

1 Play the game.

Page 104

⑨ Party clothes

1 CD2 49 **Listen and point. Then listen and say the words.**

1 hat

2 belt

4 shirt

3 boots

5 badge

6 shoes

2 CD2 50 **Listen and chant.**

1 CD2 51 **Listen and point. Choose food for a class party.**

2 Think! **Draw your five favourite foods in order.**

I like (biscuits, crisps, salad, sweets).

1 Listen and match.

2 Think! Guess the toys and stick.

Sticker

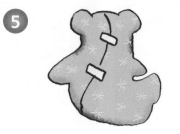

I've got (apples and salad / a ball). 93

Nice work!

1

2

3

4

5

6

7

8

2 Think! Find and say the picture number.

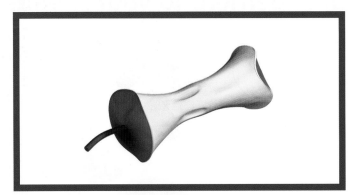

Our clothes

1 CD2 57 Listen and say the number.

1   2   3   4

2 Draw clothes. Show your superhero to your friends.

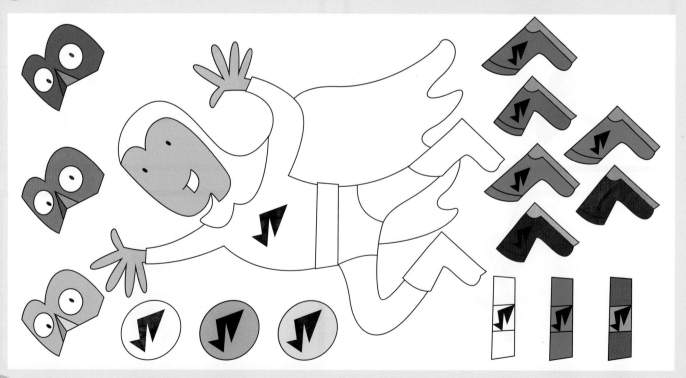

1 (Think!) **Look at the numbers. Colour the uniforms.**

| 1 | 2 | 3 | 4 | 5 | 6 | 7 | 8 | 9 | 10 |

2 **Draw and colour a new school uniform.**

1 Play the game.

Chants and songs

What's your name? (page 4)

What's your name? What's your name?
 I'm Mike.
Hello Mike.

What's your name? What's your name?
 I'm Polly.
Hello Polly.

What's your name? What's your name?
 I'm Leo.
Hello Leo.

What's your name? What's your name?
 I'm Gina.
Hello Gina.

Gina, Polly, Mike and Leo,
Hello, hello, hello, hello!

My pencil (page 10)

My pencil, my book, my rubber –
All in my bag.

My pencil, my book, my rubber –
All on my chair.

My pencil, my book, my rubber –
All on my desk.

In the classroom (page 12)

In the classroom, in the classroom.
In the classroom, today!
Here's my rubber, my red rubber.
Here's my rubber in my pencil case!

In the classroom ...
Here's my pencil, my blue pencil.
Here's my pencil in my pencil case!

In the classroom ...
My rubber and my pencil,
My rubber and my pencil,
My rubber and my pencil
In my pencil case.

In my family (page 20)

My grandma, my sister, my mum and me.
Here are the girls in my family.

My grandpa, my brother, my dad and me.
Here are the boys in my family.

We're the royal family! (page 22)

Mum's the queen! Dad's the king!
We're the royal family! (x 2)

This is my mum.
 Hi, my name's Ann.
This is my dad.
 Hi, my name's Dan.
Mum's the queen! ...

This is my sister.
 Hi, my name's Jill.
This is my brother.
 Hi, my name's Bill.
Mum's the queen! ...

This is my grandma.
 Hi, my name's Kim.
This is my grandpa.
 Hi, my name's Jim.
Mum's the queen! ... (x 2)

Here's my face (page 30)

Here's my face. It's easy – look!
Two eyes, two ears.
Here's my nose. Here's my mouth.
Oh, what's missing? Ah – my teeth! (x 2)

Hey, little clown (page 32)

Hey, little clown. Are you happy?
Hey, little clown. Are you OK?
Hey, little clown. Are you happy?
Are you happy today?
No, no, no, no, no. I'm not happy. I'm not happy.
No, no, no, no, no. I'm sad today.

Hey, little clown …
No, no, no, no, no. I'm not happy. I'm not happy.
No, no, no, no, no. I'm scared today.

Hey, little clown …
No, no, no, no, no. I'm not happy. I'm not happy.
No, no, no, no, no. I'm angry today.

Hey, little clown …
Yes, yes, yes, yes, yes. I'm happy. I'm happy.
Yes, yes, yes, yes, yes. I'm OK today.
I'm happy today.

One yellow doll (page 40)

One yellow doll, two blue balls,
Three green planes, four red kites,
A rope and a teddy bear.
Oh yeah, oh yeah, oh yeah!

I've got a ball (page 42)

I've got a ball and a plane.
I've got a doll and a rope.
I've got a teddy bear – squawk!
I've got a teddy bear.
I haven't got a kite. I haven't got a kite.
Sob, sob, sob. I haven't got a kite. Sob, sob.

I've got a kite. That's right! That's right!
I've got a kite. That's right!
Play with me. Play with me.
I've got a kite. That's right!
　　We've got a kite. We've got a kite.
　　We've got a kite. That's right! (x 2)

Teddies everywhere! (page 50)

A teddy on the table, a teddy in the bath,
A teddy on the sofa, teddies everywhere.
A teddy on the cupboard,
A teddy on the bed,
A teddy on the armchair,
Teddies everywhere!

Tidy up! (page 52)

Tidy up, tidy up. Put your toys away! (x 2)

Put the kite in the cupboard.
Put the plane under the bed.
No more play. Put your toys away.

Tidy up …

Put the doll on the bed.
Put the teddy on the chair.
No more play. Put your toys away.

Tidy up … Put your toys away!

Listen! (page 60)

Listen! Woof, woof. A dog!
Listen! Miaow. A cat!
Listen! Baaa! A sheep!
Listen! Mooo! A cow!
Listen! Neigh! A horse!
Listen! Thump, thump! A rabbit!
Run, rabbit, run! Run, rabbit, run!
Look at the rabbit running away!

The animal boogie (page 62)

Let's do the animal boogie – woof!
Let's do the animal boogie – miaow!
Let's do the animal boogie – baaa!
Let's do the animal boogie – mooo!
Come sing with me and dance with me,
For you and me, the animal boogie-woogie!

I like dogs, oh dogs are nice!
Woof, woof, woof, woof, woof.
I like cats, oh cats are nice!
Miaow, miaow, miaow, miaow, miaow.
I like sheep, oh sheep are nice!
Baaa, baaa, baaa, baaa, baaa.
I like cows, oh cows are nice!
Mooo, mooo, mooo, mooo, mooo!
Come sing with me …

And I like the animal boogie too!
Woof! Miaow! Baaa! Mooo!
Come sing with me …

Cakes for the snakes (page 70)

Cakes for the snakes,
Apples for the cats,
Carrots for the parrots,
Ice cream for the sheep.
Sausages, sausages,
Sausages and chips!
Sausages and chips
For you and me!

I don't like chips (page 72)

I don't like chips - no, no, no.
I don't like carrots - no, no, no.
I don't like sausages - no, no, no.
No, no, no, no, NO!
Chips, oh no! Carrots, oh no!
Sausages - no, no, no, no, NO!

I like apples - yes, yes, yes.
I like cakes - yes, yes, yes.
I like ice cream - yes, yes, yes.
Yes, yes, yes, yes, YES!
Apples, oh yes! Cakes, oh yes!
Ice cream - yes, yes, yes, yes, YES!

Ride a scooter (page 80)

Ride a scooter.
Sail a boat.
Drive a car.
Off we go!

Ride a bike.
Drive a bus.
Drive a train.
Come with us!

We're having fun! (page 82)

Look at us. We're having fun!
Come and join in, everyone!

I'm riding a bike. Ting, ting, ting.
I'm driving a car. Vroom, vroom, vroom.
I'm flying a plane. Neeeaow!
I'm flying to the stars.

Look at us. We're having fun!
Come and join in, everyone! (x 2)

I'm driving a train. Choo, choo, choo.
I'm riding a scooter. Push, push!
I'm sailing a boat. All aboard!
I'm sailing on the sea.

Look at us. We're having fun!
Come and join in, everyone! (x 2)

Mike's a cowboy (page 90)

Purple shirt, blue boots,
No shoes, red belt,
Yellow badge, green hat.
Mike's a cowboy. That's that! (x 2)

Oh what a wonderful party! (page 92)

Oh what a wonderful party!
It's party time today!
Clap your hands! Turn around!
Shout 'Hip, hip, hooray!'

Sausages, sausages in my tummy.
Sausages, sausages,
Yummy, yummy, yummy!

Oh what a wonderful party!
It's party time today!
Clap your hands! Turn around!
Shout 'Hip, hip, hooray!'

Ice cream, ice cream in my tummy.
Ice cream, ice cream,
Yummy, yummy, yummy!

Oh what a wonderful party!
It's party time today!
Clap your hands! Turn around!
Shout 'Hip, hip, hooray!'
Shout 'Hip, hip, hooray!'

Unit 7 Game (page 79)

Unit 8 Game (page 89)

Unit 4 Game (page 49)

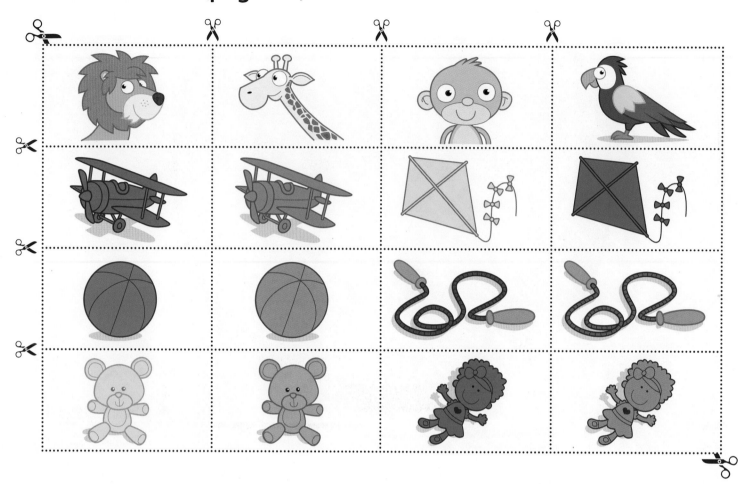

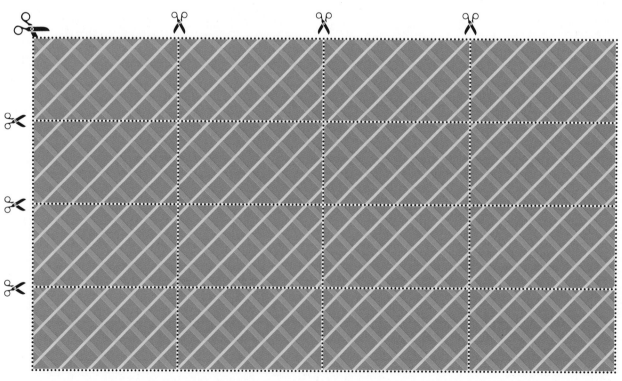

Unit 2 Game (page 29)

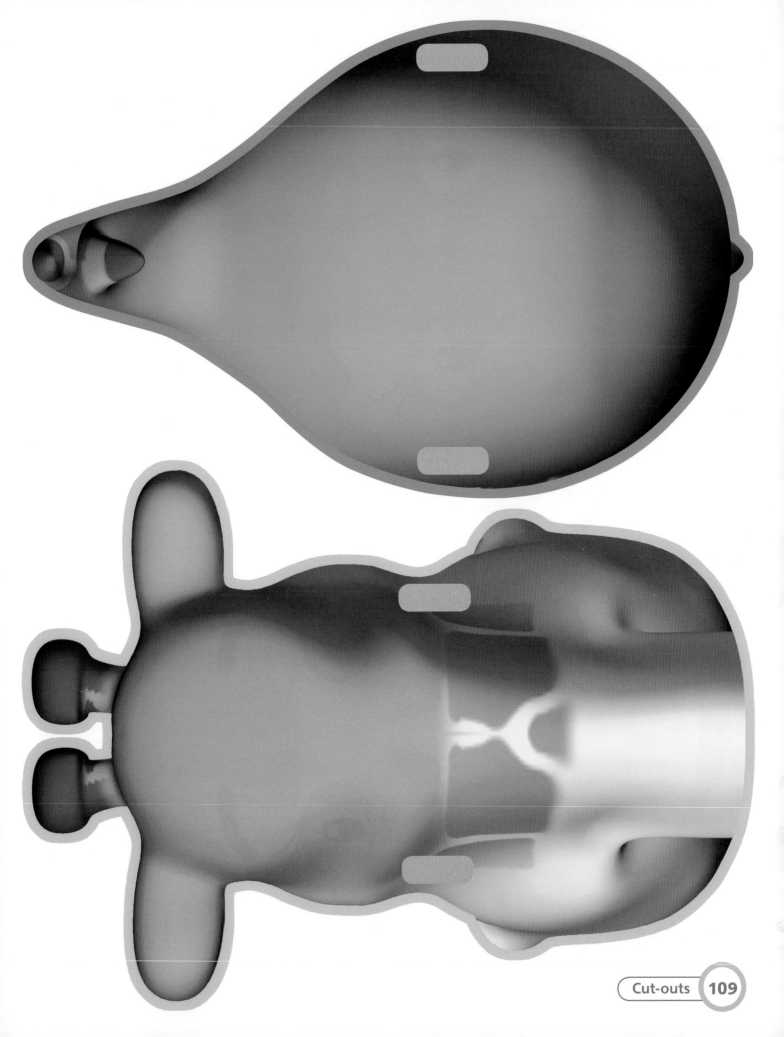

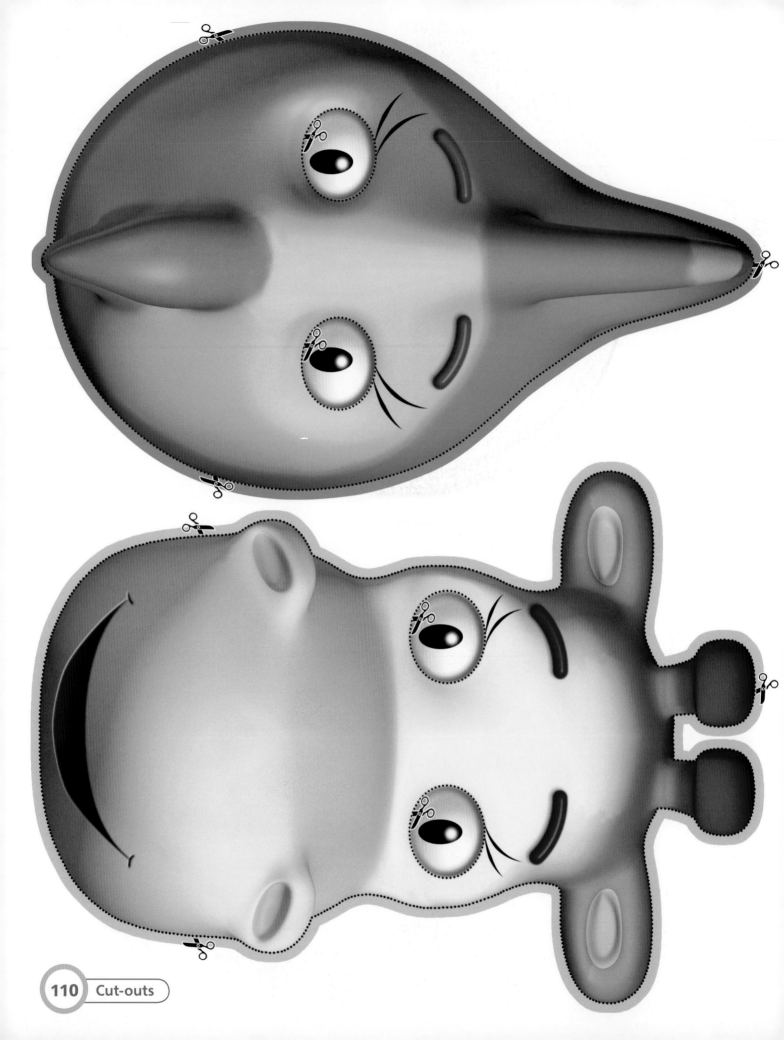

1 2 3 4 5 6